20 FUN FACTS ABOUT THE INDUSTRIAL REVOLUTION

By Joan Stoltman

Gareth Stevens
PUBLISHING

Please visit our website, www.garethstevens.com. For a free color catalog of all our high-quality books, call toll free 1-800-542-2595 or fax 1-877-542-2596.

Library of Congress Cataloging-in-Publication Data
Names: Stoltman, Joan, author.
Title: 20 fun facts about the industrial revolution / Joan Stoltman.
Description: New York : Gareth Stevens Publishing, [2019] | Series: Fun fact
  file: US history! | Includes index.
Identifiers: LCCN 2018003841| ISBN 9781538219133 (library bound) | ISBN
  9781538219119 (pbk.) | ISBN 9781538219126 (6 pack)
Subjects: LCSH: Industrial revolution–United States–History.
Classification: LCC HC105 .S86 2018 | DDC 330.973/05–dc23
LC record available at https://lccn.loc.gov/2018003841

Published in 2019 by
Gareth Stevens Publishing
111 East 14th Street, Suite 349
New York, NY 10003

Copyright © 2019 Gareth Stevens Publishing

Designer: Sarah Liddell
Editor: Mariel Bard

Photo credits: Cover, p. 1 Mondadori Portfolio/Contributor/Mondadori Portfolio/
Getty Images; p. 5 Scewing/Wikimedia Commons; p. 6 Mzilikazi1939/Wikimedia Commons; p. 7
Print Collector/Contributor/Hulton Archive/Getty Images; p. 8 Andy Dingley/
Wikimedia Commons; p. 9 Ipsumpix/Contributor/Corbis Historical/Getty Images;
p. 10 Stahlkocher/Wikimedia Commons; p. 11 Rischgitz/Stringer/Hulton Archive/
Getty Images; p. 12 Marcbela/Wikimedia Commons; p. 13 Scartol/Wikimedia Commons;
p. 14 Science & Society Picture Library/Contributor/SSPL/Getty Images; p. 15 Bubamara/
Wikimedia Commons; pp. 16, 19, 29 (camera then) Bettmann/Contributor/Bettmann/
Getty Images; p. 17 Rmhermen/Wikimedia Commons; p. 18 Nancy Nehring/Contributor/Moment
Mobile/Getty Images; p. 20 Beyond My Ken/Wikimedia Commons;
p. 21 Nconwaymicelli/Wikimedia Commons; p. 22 GraphicaArtis/Contributor/Archive Photos/
Getty Images; p. 23 Steinsplitter Bot/Wikimedia Commons; p. 24 Globalphilosophy/Wikimedia
Commons; p. 25 George Rinhart/Contributor/Corbis Historical/Getty Images;
p. 27 Everett Historical/Shutterstock.com; p. 28 (safety pin then) Doug Coldwell/
Wikimedia Commons; p. 28 (safety pin now) Gayvoronskaya_Yana/Shutterstock.com;
p. 28 (QWERTY keyboard then and telephone then) Chetvorno/Wikimedia Commons;
p. 28 (QWERTY keyboard now) Runish/Shutterstock.com; p. 28 (telephone now) Cropbot/
Wikimedia Commons; p. 29 (camera now) erashov/Shutterstock.com; p. 29 (sewing machine
then) Pigsonthewing/Wikimedia Commons; p. 29 (sewing machine now) Africa Studio/
Shutterstock.com.

Printed in the United States of America

CPSIA compliance information: Batch #CS18GS: For further information contact Gareth Stevens, New York, New York at 1-800-542-2595.

Contents

Words in the glossary appear in **bold** type the first time they are used in the text.

Big Changes!

Before the Industrial Revolution, families would grow, build, and make everything they needed to survive. This included food, clothing, furniture, and even toys. But life began to change, first in Great Britain around 1760 and then in the United States.

"Industrial" refers to factories, machines, and how things are made. A revolution is a big, sudden change. The Industrial Revolution was a major change in the **production** of everyday goods. New machines were invented to increase production in factories. The ways people worked, learned, traveled, ate, and even talked to each other would never be the same.

Before the 1760s, most people in Great Britain and the United States lived and worked on farms or in small towns. They didn't usually travel far from the town where they were born.

FACT 1

The power of the British Empire created perfect conditions for the Industrial Revolution to begin.

During the 18th century, Great Britain was a powerful empire with colonies around the world, including in America. It also had **natural resources**, such as coal, that would become very important during the Industrial Revolution.

The Industrial Revolution in Great Britain quickly changed how the country looked, with cities growing and factories being built. The population also grew!

"Jenny" was a shorter way to say "engine." The spinning jenny became one of the most useful machines of the century!

FACT 2

A machine called the spinning jenny helped kick off the Industrial Revolution!

The spinning jenny was invented in Britain in 1764 by James Hargreaves. This machine could make more than one ball of thread at a time, which sped up the production of **textiles**, including clothes.

Powered by Steam

FACT 3

The coal industry boomed because of the steam engine!

Thomas Newcomen's steam engine, invented in Britain in 1712, pumped water out of flooded coal mines. James Watt of Scotland improved Newcomen's engine in the 1760s. Now miners could dig deeper for more coal—which meant more power for more machines!

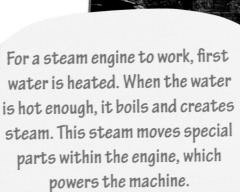

NEWCOMEN PUMPING ENGINE NEAR ASHTON UNDER LYNE

For a steam engine to work, first water is heated. When the water is hot enough, it boils and creates steam. This steam moves special parts within the engine, which powers the machine.

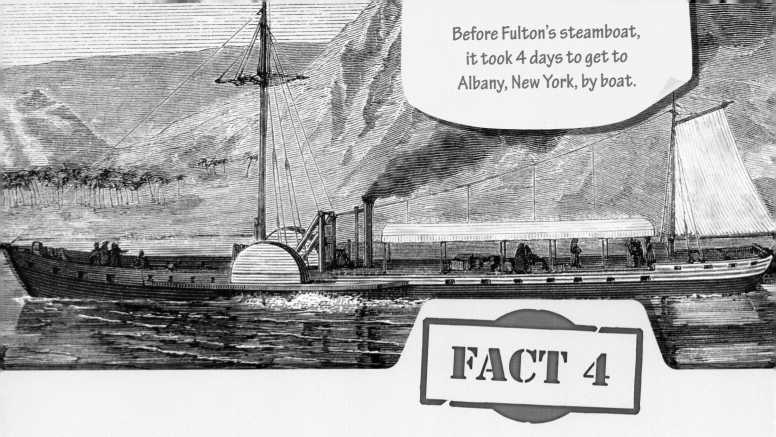

Before Fulton's steamboat, it took 4 days to get to Albany, New York, by boat.

FACT 4

Robert Fulton's steamboat went just 4.7 miles (7.6 km) an hour—but that was fast back then!

Fulton's steamboat traveled up the Hudson River for the first time on August 17, 1807. The trip from New York City to Albany was 150 miles (241 km) and took only 32 hours.

The man who built America's first steam-powered train also ran for president!

Peter Cooper had big ideas and a drive to make them happen. He built a small train called the Tom Thumb. On August 28, 1830, the Tom Thumb ran on the Baltimore and Ohio (or B&O) Railroad for the first time, carrying 40 people.

Cooper ran for president in 1876, but he didn't win. Instead, Rutherford B. Hayes was elected.

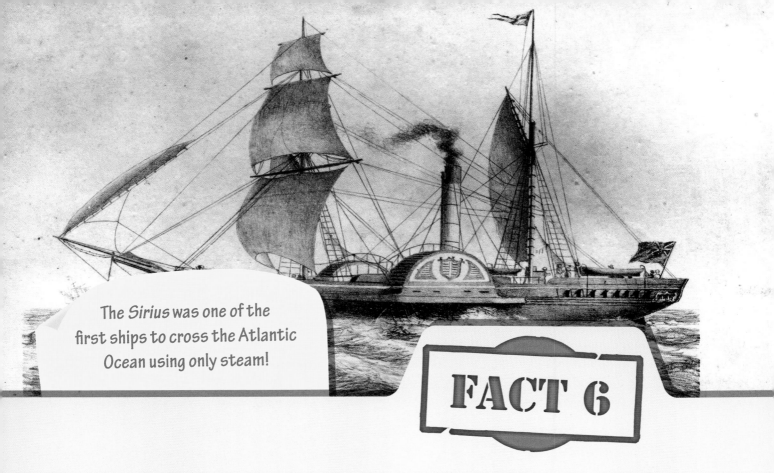

The *Sirius* was one of the first ships to cross the Atlantic Ocean using only steam!

FACT 6

A steamship crew burned furniture to finish the trip across the Atlantic Ocean!

Big steam-powered ships were better for longer journeys because they were much faster than sailing. In 1838, a ship called the *Sirius* ran out of coal. The captain refused to use the ship's sails, so the crew burned furniture to finish the trip!

FACT 7

The "father of the American factory system" built textile machines from memory!

Slatersville Mill

Samuel Slater was from Britain, but he wanted to build textile mills in America. Britain wouldn't let him take written plans when he left in 1789, so he memorized them.

In 1790, Slater's first textile mill was running in Pawtucket, Rhode Island. By 1803, he and his brother opened Slatersville, Rhode Island, a whole village built around a big mill.

By 1840, about 8,000 women worked in Lowell's mills.

The town of Lowell, Massachusetts, was designed for making textiles!

Francis Cabot Lowell ran the first textile mill in America that could turn raw cotton into textiles all in one factory. After Lowell died, a new town was named for him and more textile mills were built.

The sewing machine was invented in America, but no one wanted to build it!

Elias Howe took his **patented** invention to Britain instead. In 1849, when Howe came back to America, he found Isaac Singer selling a machine just like his. Howe took Singer to court in 1854 and won.

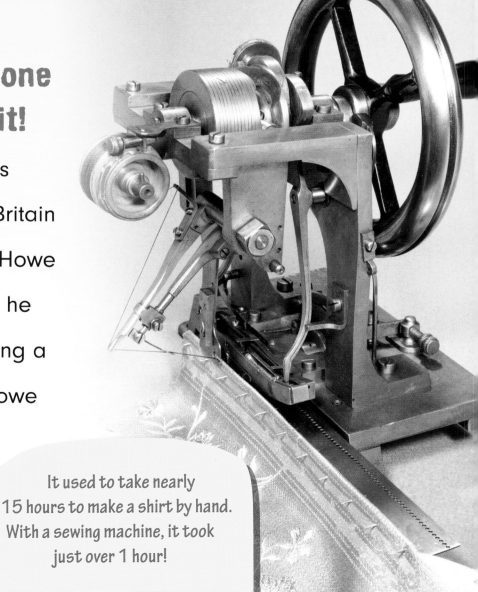

It used to take nearly 15 hours to make a shirt by hand. With a sewing machine, it took just over 1 hour!

FACT 10

Children as young as 6 years old worked in factories.

Many children took jobs during the Industrial Revolution, and child labor become a major problem. Children were paid very little and worked long hours. Conditions within the factories were often dangerous.

Workers could get their arms and legs caught in fast-moving machine parts. They also breathed in smoke that was bad for their health.

FACT 11

Eli Whitney thought he'd get rich after inventing the cotton gin, but no one wanted to pay for it!

Whitney's cotton gin easily separated cotton seeds from cotton fiber, which used to take a long time when done by hand. However, instead of buying his machine, people just began making their own.

"One man and a horse will do more than 50 men with the old machine," Whitney wrote of his invention.

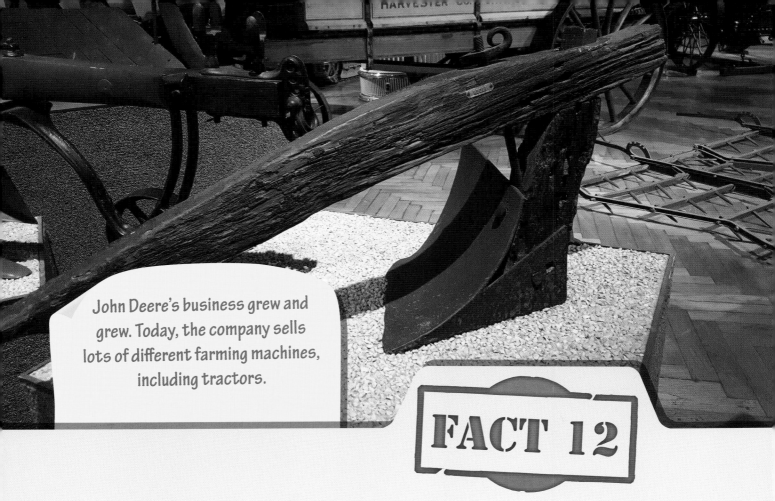

John Deere's business grew and grew. Today, the company sells lots of different farming machines, including tractors.

FACT 12

The first item John Deere sold was a plow!

In 1837, John Deere made a plow with sharp steel blades that cut through hard, sticky soil without needing a lot of cleaning. This made farming easier and saved a lot of time.

Grain elevators moved more grain in 2 hours than people moved in a day!

Steam-powered grain elevators were first built in 1842 to solve problems with storing and moving grain. These tall buildings could hold lots of grain, which was then loaded onto a ship or a train to be sold elsewhere.

Grain elevators were filled with corn, wheat, oats, or other grains.

FACT 14

An immigrant from Scotland created the American steel industry!

At age 13, Andrew Carnegie moved to America with his family. As an adult, he saw how important steel was to railroads, buildings, and bridges. Carnegie opened his first steel **plant** in 1875. Using new methods to make steel cheaper, his company became very successful.

Carnegie sold his steel company for $480 million in 1901, which would equal about $14 billion today. That made him the richest man in the world.

19

The first skyscraper was only 10 stories high!

Designed by William Le Baron Jenney, the Home Insurance Building of Chicago, Illinois, was finished in 1885. It was the first building to use a steel frame. Steel allowed buildings to be built taller than ever before.

Steel made skyscrapers lighter and sturdier. If the Home Insurance Building had been made of stone, it would have weighed three times as much!

A Big Deal

Cannons announced the opening of the Erie Canal in 1825!

The canal ran 363 miles (584 km), connecting Lake Erie and the Hudson River. Cannons were set up all along the canal, and they started firing when the first boat left Buffalo, New York, headed for Albany, New York.

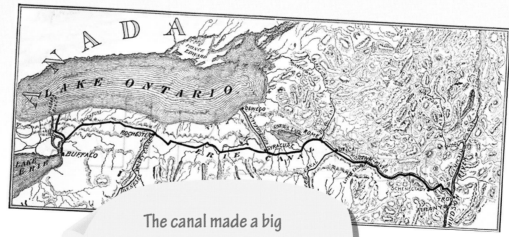

The canal made a big difference in how goods, such as grain, could be brought from the Midwest to the East Coast. A trip that used to take 2 weeks by land now took only 5 days.

FACT 17

Four special **spikes**—including two made of gold—joined the two halves of the transcontinental railroad.

To connect the East Coast and the West Coast, one railroad company started laying tracks in California, and another company started work near Omaha, Nebraska. They met at Promontory Summit in the Utah Territory on May 10, 1869.

In 1840, America had only 3,000 miles (4,828 km) of railroad. By 1916, it had 254,000 miles (408,773 km)!

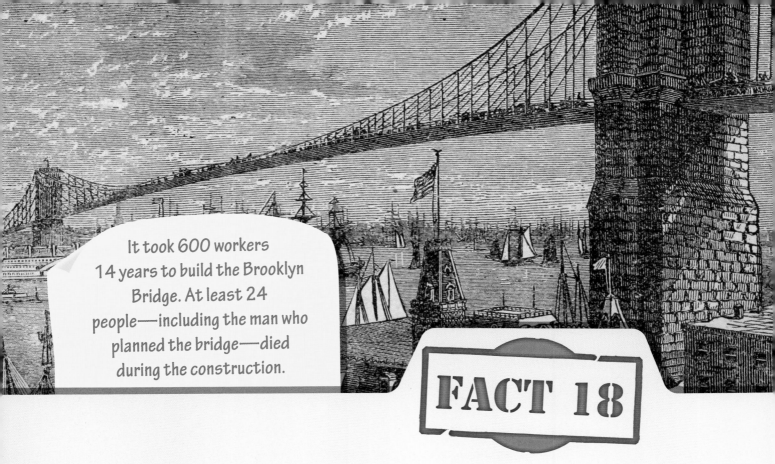

It took 600 workers 14 years to build the Brooklyn Bridge. At least 24 people—including the man who planned the bridge—died during the construction.

FACT 18

Elephants walked on the Brooklyn Bridge!

When it opened on May 24, 1883, the Brooklyn Bridge was the first steel-wire **suspension bridge** in the world. But people were nervous about crossing it, so in 1884, circus showman P. T. Barnum marched 21 elephants across the bridge to prove its strength!

FACT 19

The telephone has more than one inventor!

Though Alexander Graham Bell is known as the inventor of the telephone, there were at least two other people who had the same idea. Antonio Meucci and Elisha Gray both tried to tell the world about their inventions, but Bell was awarded the patent on February 14, 1876.

In 2002, Congress officially recognized Meucci as the inventor of the telephone. Meucci had created his telephone in 1860—16 years before Bell.

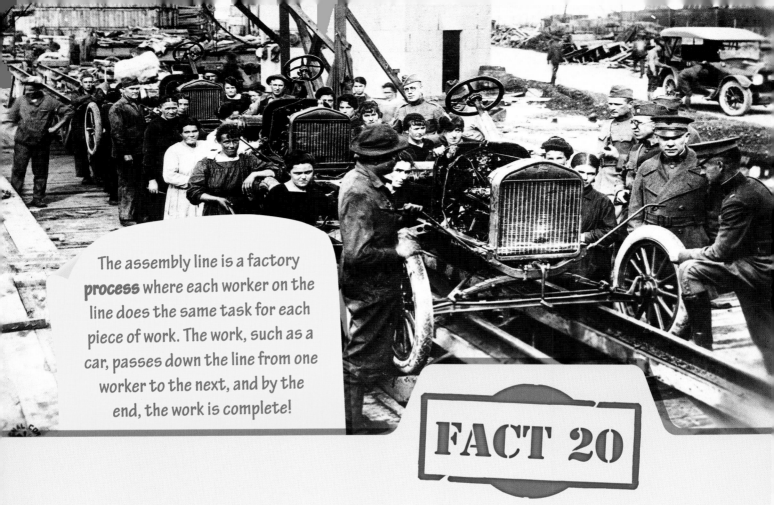

The assembly line is a factory **process** where each worker on the line does the same task for each piece of work. The work, such as a car, passes down the line from one worker to the next, and by the end, the work is complete!

FACT 20

Henry Ford didn't invent the assembly line!

It was originally thought up by Ransom E. Olds (founder of Oldsmobile) in 1901. Ford perfected the moving assembly line and made it famous by reducing the time spent making a car from more than 12 hours to just 93 minutes by 1914!

It's a Revolution!

The Industrial Revolution changed the way people lived and worked forever. Among the biggest changes during this time period was the largest population growth in human history. In 1700, there were fewer than 700 million people on Earth. By 1900, that number was about 1.6 billion!

In many ways, the Industrial Revolution created modern America. We still use many of the inventions created all those years ago. Just imagine how different your life would be without lightbulbs, cars, and telephones!

The Industrial Revolution created lots of new jobs. Many people moved from the countryside, where they grew up, to cities, where they took jobs in factories.

Still Used Today

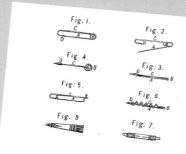

THEN (1849)

SAFETY PIN

NOW

THEN (1873)

THEN (1876)

TELEPHONE

NOW

NOW

Many amazing and useful products were invented during the Industrial Revolution. Today, they might look a little different than they did more than 100 years ago. People continue to improve the original inventions.

THEN (1844)

SEWING MACHINE

NOW

THEN (1888)

CAMERA

NOW

Glossary

canal: a man-made waterway

immigrant: one who comes to a country to settle there

industry: the process of making products using machines and factories

natural resource: something in nature that can be used by people

patent: having to with obtaining an official document that gives a person the rights to a product for a time

plant: a building or factory where something is made

plow: a farm machine that is used to dig into and turn over soil

process: a series of steps or actions taken to complete something

production: the process of making something for sale or use

skyscraper: a very tall building in a city

spike: a long, thin rod that ends in a point and is often made of metal

suspension bridge: a bridge with a road held by two or more cables usually passing over towers and strongly held down at the ends

textile: cloth that is woven or knit

For More Information

Books

Brasch, Nicolas. *The Industrial Revolution: Age of Invention*. New York, NY: PowerKids Press, 2014.

Garstecki, Julia. *Life During the Industrial Revolution*. Minneapolis, MN: ABDO Publishing Group, 2015.

Mooney, Carla. *Perspectives on the Industrial Revolution*. Mankato, MN: 12-Story Library, 2018.

Websites

Industrial Revolution
www.history.com/topics/industrial-revolution/videos/the-industrial-revolution
See how the American way of life changed with the Industrial Revolution.

Industrial Supremacy
www.learner.org/series/biographyofamerica/prog14/feature/index.html
Learn more about the incredible inventions of the Industrial Revolution with this interactive timeline.

Index